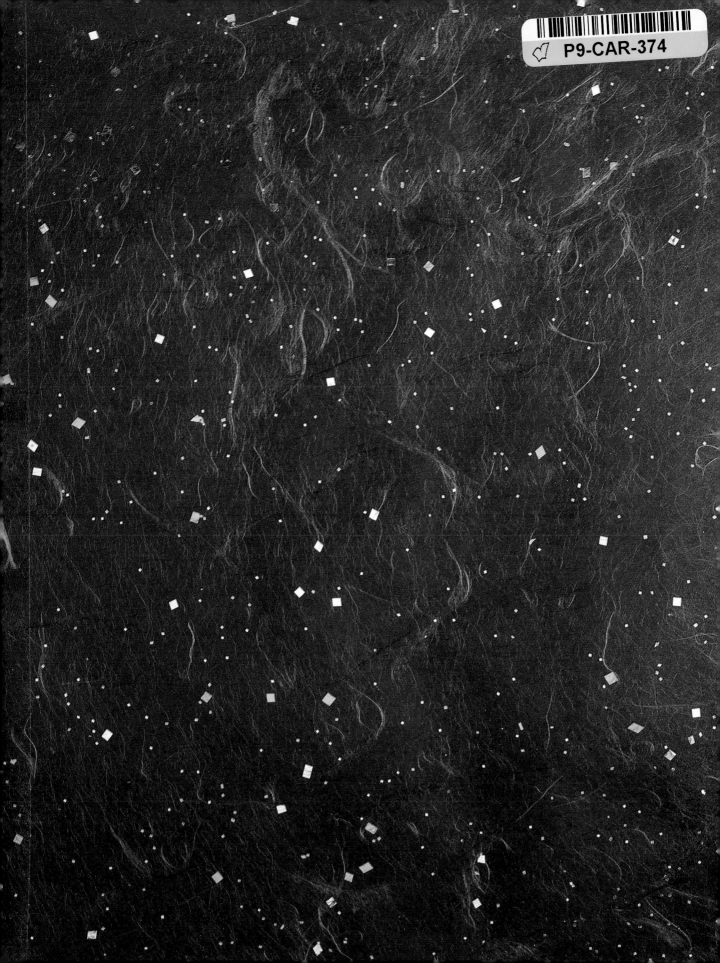

Burglind Niermann

Great Gift Wrapping

Sterling Publishing Co., Inc.   New York

Library of Congress Cataloging-in-Publication Data

Niermann, Burglind.
    Great gift wrapping.

    Translation of: Deco Art.
    Includes index.
    1. Gift wrapping.   I. Title.
TT870.N5213   1989   745.54   89-11492
ISBN 0-8069-5766-2
ISBN 0-8069-5767-0 (pbk.)

Translated by Elizabeth Reinersmann

English translation copyright © 1989
by Sterling Publishing Co., Inc.
387 Park Avenue South, New York, N.Y. 10016
Original edition published under the title: "Deco Art:
Die Kunst, Geschenke zu verpacken." © 1988 by
Falken-Verlag GmbH, Niedernhausen/TS., West Germany
Distributed in Canada by Sterling Publishing
% Canadian Manda Group, P.O. Box 920, Station U
Toronto, Ontario, Canada M8Z 5P9
Distributed in Great Britain and Europe by Cassell PLC
Artillery House, Artillery Row, London SW1P 1RT, England
Distributed in Australia by Capricorn Ltd.
P.O. Box 665, Lane Cove, NSW 2066
Manufactured in the United States of America
All rights reserved

CONTENTS

Introduction 6

Materials 8
    Paper 10
    Ribbons 10
    Tools 11

Sweets for My Sweet 12
    Simple but Original:
    Wrapping Small Packages 14

Paper 16
    Folding, Shaping,
    Experimenting 17
    Folding, Creasing, Crunching 18
    The Fan 20
    The Accordion 22

A Parade of Bows 24
    Making Your Own Bows 26

Bows Made in Different Materials 29
    Paper Bows 30
    Butterfly 31
    A Soft Touch 31
    Placing a Bow 32

Bottle Parade 34
    Hiding Bottles 36
    The Individual Touch 38
    Two Bottles in a Blanket 40

Wrap It in a Shirt! 42
    Dressing up a Bottle 44
    A Bottle in a Tuxedo 46

Accessories 48
    Decorations for Every
    Occasion 50

Bachelor Party 53

Cherry Blossom Time 54
    Spring Is Here! 56

It's Christmas 58
    Wrapping for Christmas 60

Easter Eggs 62
    Easter Bows 64
    Emphasis on Feathers 65

Wedding Bells Are Ringing 66

Congratulations! 68

For the Young Adult 71

Daring Colors 72

Red and Black 74

New York, New York 76

American Life 78

Index 80

Introduction

A new concept in gift giving is that of letting our imaginations fly when it comes to wrapping gifts for our friends and loved ones. The concept of gift-wrapping as an art form seems to have evolved and is here to stay. Taking gift-wrapping to its highest level means more than just wrapping presents in a new and fanciful way; it also includes the way in which the table or the room is decorated to enhance the festive occasion. Regardless of whether a present is for a birthday, a wedding, or for Christmas, we do not need to just wrap the box in paper and stick a bow on top. Now we are able to lavishly demonstrate our creativity. People are creating wonderful surprises—even before the packages are opened! A whole profession has sprung up around this activity. With this book the art form is also available to amateurs.

The only limitations, from the choice of materials to color combinations, are those that the individual brings to the task. Be daring, therefore, in the way in which you make use of paper, bows, ribbons and lace as well as all the other now easily available and vastly expanded decorating materials.

To prepare for this book, I searched high and low—I looked at all the different ways in which presents are wrapped in the Orient as well as in the West. I found nothing in writing. No instructions of any kind have been handed down as to how to use deco-rative accessories to turn an ordinarily wrapped present into something special: a work of art. I believe that the examples presented in this book will guide the imagination and bring a new standard of beauty to this art form.

The inspiration for this book came from my customers. They never stopped being enthusiastic about what I was doing and freely expressed their amazement over my creations. Encouraged, I attempt here to share what I have learned with all those who want to have more fun wrapping their presents.

Materials

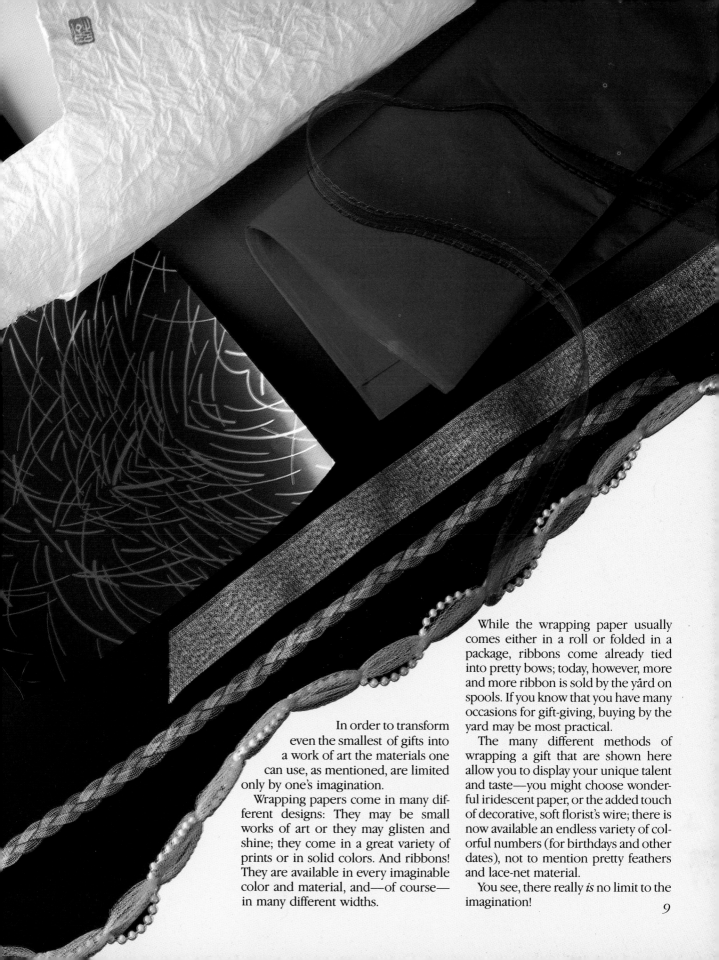

In order to transform even the smallest of gifts into a work of art the materials one can use, as mentioned, are limited only by one's imagination.

Wrapping papers come in many different designs: They may be small works of art or they may glisten and shine; they come in a great variety of prints or in solid colors. And ribbons! They are available in every imaginable color and material, and—of course— in many different widths.

While the wrapping paper usually comes either in a roll or folded in a package, ribbons come already tied into pretty bows; today, however, more and more ribbon is sold by the yard on spools. If you know that you have many occasions for gift-giving, buying by the yard may be most practical.

The many different methods of wrapping a gift that are shown here allow you to display your unique talent and taste—you might choose wonderful iridescent paper, or the added touch of decorative, soft florist's wire; there is now available an endless variety of colorful numbers (for birthdays and other dates), not to mention pretty feathers and lace-net material.

You see, there really *is* no limit to the imagination!

9

Paper

As a rule it is not difficult to find wrapping paper. for your projects. Make a collection of them! Here is a list of some wrapping papers with comments on their characteristics:

- Ordinary printed wrapping paper is universally available and will accommodate almost all your needs.
- Tissue paper is soft and handles oddly shaped packages well. It is easy to crumble and when flattened again has a casual look. Wadded up, it can cushion fragile gifts or disguise recognizable shapes, but when used as the exterior wrapping it does not hold sharp folds or tolerate prolonged handling.
- Brown package- or packing-paper is a fun way to hide your gift and to create all kinds of shapes with sharp folds and creases that will stay put.
- Plastic-coated paper is easy to cut, has edges that won't tear and is waterproof. Your gift will be impressive and elegant.

- Metallic paper or paper coated with clear sealer and/or metallic coating are not as easy to handle due to their stiffness—folds must be perfect on the first attempt or creases from repeated attempts will show. But metallics provide wonderfully dramatic effects.

Ribbons

Again—as with wrapping paper—ribbons come in many different materials that can make your project unique.

- Net-lace or mesh ribbons add elegance and a very soft, romantic touch to your project.

- Lurex ribbon has an interesting property: If it is held between the thumb and the edge of a scissors-blade and the blade is quickly pulled along the ribbon, the ribbon will crimp and form ringlets and cascading spirals. Several of these used together can substitute for ready-made bows.
- Silk, brocade, and satin ribbons and ribbons with printed motifs make wonderful bows.
- Plastic-coated ribbon material makes fancy ringlets also, and if a wide-width ribbon is used, it can be easily split and turned into cascades of ringlets.
- Metallic ribbons make wonderful bows and will survive long trips in the mail or in the car in good shape.

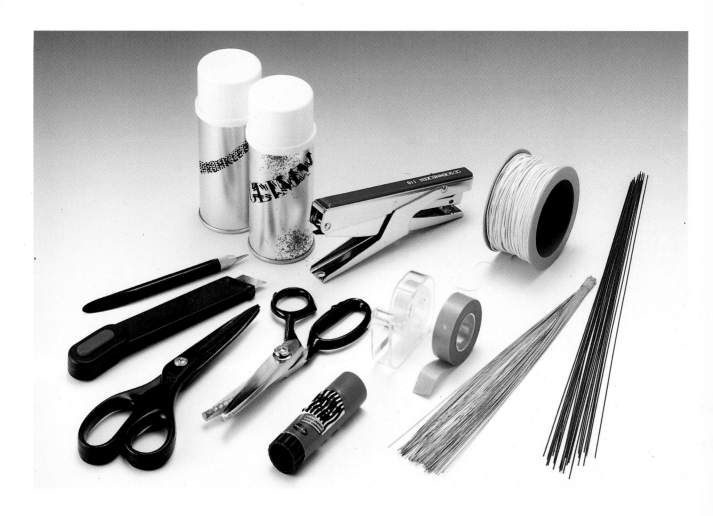

Tools

Gift-wrapping does not require a large investment in basic tools. You may have many of these items already, but some may require a trip to a specialized art-supply shop.

- Use a sharp utility-knife or scissors to cut paper. Long-bladed scissors are better than short-bladed scissors in achieving a smooth, straight cut. Long cuts made with a utility-knife should be made against a ruler or straight-edge to guarantee a straight cut.
- Pinking shears (at left corner of photo) can be useful in achieving a special zigzag effect when cutting paper.

- Double-sided transparent tape will enable you to invisibly hold the wrapping paper closed. Instead of putting single-sided tape on the outside of the seam as usual, try putting the double-sided tape on the inside lip of the top piece of wrapping paper and smoothing it down. No more distracting tape on the outside of the package!
- Attach confetti, glitter, feathers and other accessories with spray glue to give your gift that special touch. Make sure the spray you use is of the fast-drying variety and that it is not toxic or flammable. But be careful: Some sprays leave a yellow film or other telltale sign. It is a good idea to test

the spray on a piece of paper and to wait a bit, since these ruinous effects may not show immediately. Carefully shield areas that you do not want to be sprayed.
- Have a stapler on hand so that you can staple your ribbons together as well as attach them to your gift box.
- Florist's wire (at right of photo) is very useful. It can be used to reinforce your ribbons, giving them a certain amount of stiffness.
- Plastic-coated wire, sold by the yard, or colorful electrician's wire can be easier to work with than florist's wire. It can be a decorative accessory in itself in wrapping your gift.

Sweets for my

Even a small candy box for your sweetheart can—with a bit of imagination—be turned into the sensation of the evening. One way is to attach the small but pretty box to an oversized bow made of metallic ribbon. This dramatic presentation is sure to catch attention. For the greatest effect in gift-wrapping, keep in mind the importance of using contrasting colors; also be imaginative in arranging and positioning the bows.

Simple but Original: Wrapping Small Packages

The gift box does not need to be wrapped tightly. One can create an optical illusion and thereby hide the contents of the box and add to the suspense of finding out what the gift is. A small present can be made to seem large, or an obvious shape like a book or record album can be disguised.

Note: Practise folds and creases on old paper to avoid wasting expensive wrapping paper.

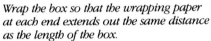

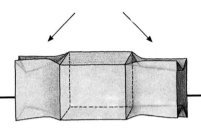

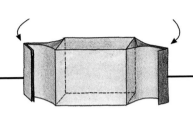

Wrap the box so that the wrapping paper at each end extends out the same distance as the length of the box.

Crease, fold and tape the paper as shown.

Fold both ends of the paper twice and fasten with tape.

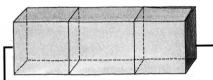

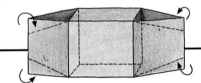

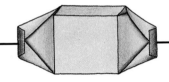

Place wrapping paper around the package as shown in the first step above.

Crease paper as shown and turn the corners in to create a more triangular shape. Fasten with tape.

Fold outer ends towards the middle and fasten with tape.

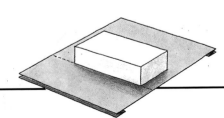

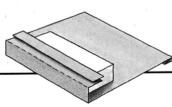

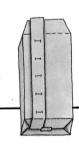

Position your box on top of the wrapping paper and accordion fold the two short sides as shown.

Fold paper as shown, making sure that the folds slide into each other, and fasten with double-sided tape.

Fold the ends in as usual and seal with tape.

Folding,
Shaping,
Experimenting

Folding, Creasing, Crunching

Here a box is held in an open-ended wrap that resembles the satchel an old-fashioned doctor took on his house calls. It is an unusual but very attractive presentation. The paper chosen for this method must take creases and must be rather strong. It is a good choice for oblong, light- or medium-weight gifts.

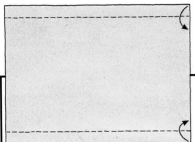

Fold your paper first along the long sides.

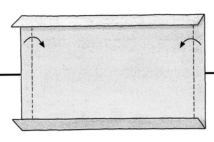

Repeat on the shorter sides.

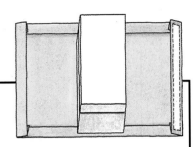

Reinforce one of these short sides with double-sided tape as shown.

Fold the paper around the gift box and join both edges along the piece of tape. Push the wrapping paper from the top

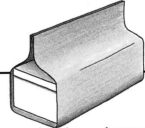

down towards the box and crease to give the appearance of a satchel. Decorate with a bow or ribbon.

It is almost impossible to hide an umbrella in a gift box. Therefore, the next best thing is to enhance the gift by wrapping it in pretty paper. Here the folds and the contrasting bows create an interesting and wonderful solution.

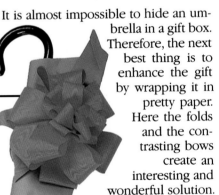

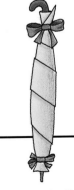

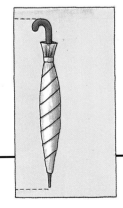

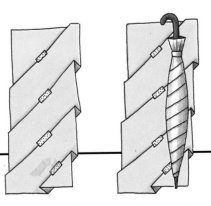

Make sure the paper is big enough to extend beyond the umbrella. Crease the paper diagonally and secure the folds

with single-sized tape on the inside as shown.

Wrap the paper around the umbrella, fasten with double-sided tape, and attach your bows.

This is a sample of a present wrapped in an unusual style. It requires a sense for the material. Beginners might want to wait before they try their hand with this one. It looks deceptively simple, but the finished product can turn out less than attractive if the crumpled pouch lacks that certain character. Practise crumbling paper that has a thin plastic or metallic coating.

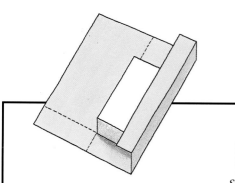

Wrap your paper around the gift box.

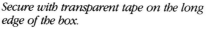

Secure with transparent tape on the long edge of the box.

Fold the ends as shown.

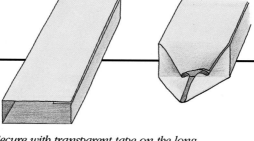

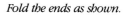

It is important to make sharp creases on every fold. Secure the folded triangles with tape.

Crumple the piece of paper that will serve as the pouch and fold it in half.

Wrap the crumpled paper around half of the box and fasten with tape.

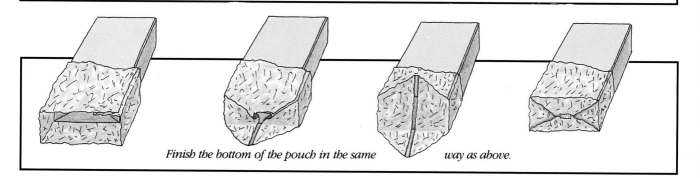

Finish the bottom of the pouch in the same way as above.

The Fan

A fan is relatively easy to make, and you will find many ways to use them. The paper is folded in accordion fashion, then the end is pinched together. Fans can be made in many different sizes and they are a wonderful means of dressing up a gift box.

Let your imagination be your guide; use one fan alone or use many, make them all from the same paper and the same size, or make them different. But they are most effective if the color of the wrapping paper and the fan is close or even the same. To liven things up one might choose contrasting colors for ribbons and bows. Wrap your gift box, as shown on page 19. Or use a ready made box to save time and paper. Whatever you use: Be imaginative in decorating your package. Don't hesitate to create your own version.

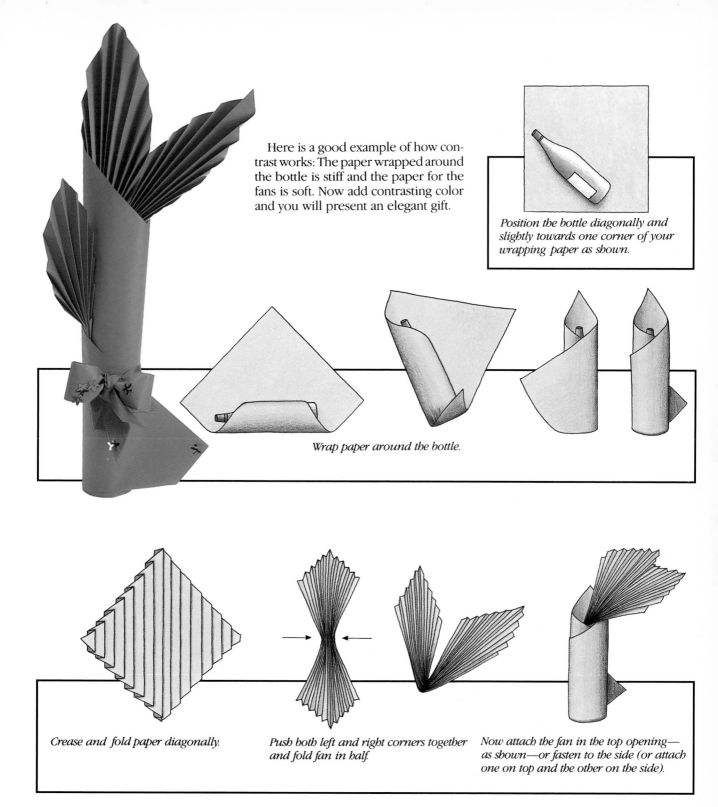

Here is a good example of how contrast works: The paper wrapped around the bottle is stiff and the paper for the fans is soft. Now add contrasting color and you will present an elegant gift.

Position the bottle diagonally and slightly towards one corner of your wrapping paper as shown.

Wrap paper around the bottle.

Crease and fold paper diagonally.

Push both left and right corners together and fold fan in half.

Now attach the fan in the top opening— as shown—or fasten to the side (or attach one on top and the other on the side).

Attach bows in contrasting colors.

The Accordion

Here is another interesting variation of the use of accordion pleats. The combination of a simple wrap for the bottle with the accordion pleats dressing up the front is very stylish. The final product displays not only your vivid imagination but also attests to your manual dexterity. It goes without saying that the paper must be rather stiff. Otherwise the folds of the accordion will not keep their shape.

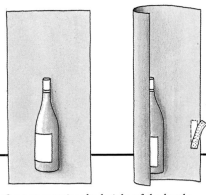

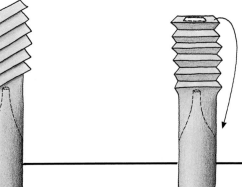

Cut paper twice the height of the bottle; attach double-sided transparent tape to the inner edge.

Wrap paper tightly around the bottle and fasten with the tape.

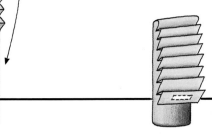

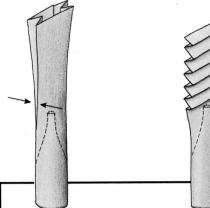

Crease the portion of the paper that extends beyond the top of the bottle and fold sides, as shown, to flatten the top.

Crease and fold this top portion of the paper in accordion fashion.

Attach a piece of the double-sided tape to the top, fold this whole pleated piece down over the bottle, and fasten to it.

Note: Be exact when making folds and creases. The overall appearance depends on it. Finish with a wide ribbon and bow in a contrasting color.

Decorate your creation with a contrasting ribbon, a bow, as well as some glitter and/ or feathers.

Of course, what looks good around a bottle will be just as pretty for any other gift box; use this method for records, small boxes of jewelry, and the like. A small gift will look particularly impressive when the accordion method is used.

Note: If the wrapping paper is not big enough, wrap your gift the conventional way and make an accordion out of a separate piece of paper. It works just as well.

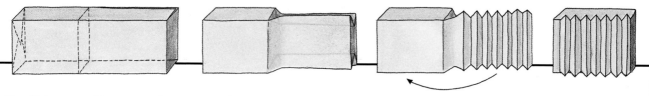

The gift is wrapped in a piece of paper a little more than twice the length of the box, as shown. Fold one end flat as shown on page 19.

The paper that extends beyond the box is creased and folded flat.

This extension is creased and folded in accordion fashion, pulled back across the box and fastened with tape.

A Parade of Bows

The bow is the crowning touch to any gift that is wrapped with imagination and love. They can be huge, shimmering with elegance, they can be geometrically arranged or they can point in different directions. It does not matter if they are plain or as bright as a peacock feather: They will give your gift that unique character you desire.

The way your bows are made, combined with the many decorations that can be attached to them, will transform any ordinary gift box into a work of art. Your success will not only depend on the way you tie your bow but also on the shape you will give to it. Since ribbon material is available by the yard, bows can be both pretty and inexpensive.

Making Your Own Bows

The more difficult bows require a certain manual dexterity. In addition, a good eye for the length of ribbon needed for a given bow is helpful. But all this comes with practice. The finished bow is tied together with either string or thread, sometimes with wire, and the ends are hidden inside the bow.

Don't hesitate to ask for help. Not only will it be easier to tie your bows, it will also be lot of fun.

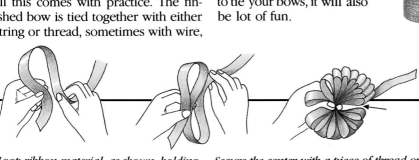

Loop ribbon material, as shown, holding the center with your thumb and index finger.

Secure the center with a piece of thread or fine decorating wire.

The Fan Bow is unquestionably the easiest bow to make, as well as the most inexpensive. If a coated ribbon material with a good "body" is used, the bow can be made big and fanciful. Again—practise makes perfect.

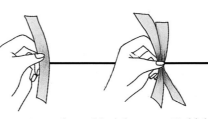

Cut ribbon in pieces of equal length, cutting the ends on the diagonal; position these pieces on top of each other, as shown.

Hold them together with thumb and index finger, as shown.

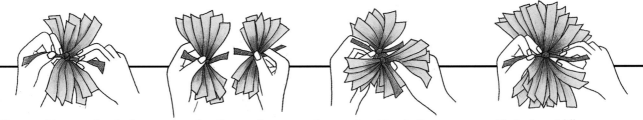

Tie everything together in the center and secure it with a string or soft wire.

Repeat above procedure and position both on top of each other.

Tie in the middle.

This elegant bow is made from ribbon material ¾-inch wide (1.9 cm). The effect is achieved by tying a simple bow and using a separate piece of ribbon for the center loop. Several bows combined create extra-large bows if that is what you are looking for. You don't need any additional decoration to achieve a smashing effect.

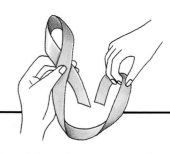

Form 2 loops from a piece of ribbon about 15½ inches long (40 cm), holding them together with thumb and index finger.

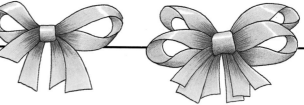

Tie your bow together with a small piece of thread.

Cover the knot with a piece of ribbon, as shown.

These two bows tied on top of each other and, again, covered with ribbon.

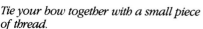

Form a loop and hold it together with thumb and index finger.

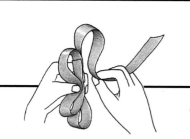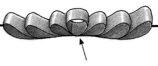

Continue forming loops but make sure that each one is a little larger than the one before. Hold loops together with

thumb and index finger and tie them together with thread or soft wire. This bow is attached across and on top of the first one. Start with a small circular

loop, the beginning of which remains inside the loop. Continue with the rest as described before. Position the second bow across the first and staple the two together.

To create a big, flower-like bow, you need "only" lots of ribbon, a very precise looping technique, but not as much patience as you would expect. The best material is plastic-coated ribbon, which comes either very shiny or satiny smooth and is sold in every conceivable color and texture.

Don't buy or use mesh-like material unless it is very stiff, because your "flower" will just collapse.

Roll your ribbon in an even circle, holding it as shown.

Press together in the middle and cut the ribbon on both sides, as shown.

Tie everything tightly together with a separate piece of ribbon.

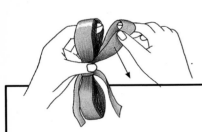 

Begin to pull out one loop at a time, starting with the top loop and alternate pulling one loop forward and the next one towards the back.

This is a variation: Alternately cut every other loop at an angle, as shown. The tip of the ribbon will extend next to a loop.

Some very artistically inclined people extend this idea. They cut the loops at a very steep angle and in an irregular fashion, creating an oriental look. Other people create fanciful peacock-like bows that are very often enhanced by the use of fanciful ribbon material.

Bows Made in Different Materials

Here are two wonderful, large bouquetlike decorating pieces, which combine a variety of materials and sizes.

The blue creation on the left is made out of the following materials: Paper, lace-net, foil, and metallic—as well as lace-net ribbons. The bows are made separately and then tied together with twine or soft wire to create one large bouquet.

The arrangement of the yellow bouquet is an example of how well contrasting materials work together when the colors are properly coordinated. For instance, an elegant and transparent lace-net is contrasted with a shiny ribbon of satin and narrow polka dot fabric. Of course, the feather in the center (attached with soft wire) really is "the dot on the i."

Paper Bows

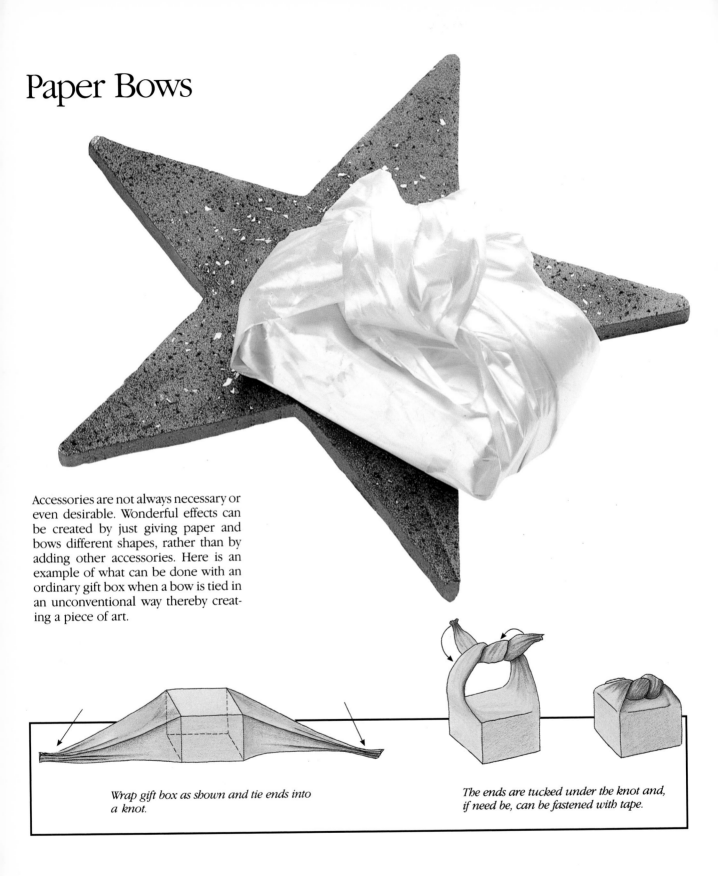

Accessories are not always necessary or even desirable. Wonderful effects can be created by just giving paper and bows different shapes, rather than by adding other accessories. Here is an example of what can be done with an ordinary gift box when a bow is tied in an unconventional way thereby creating a piece of art.

Wrap gift box as shown and tie ends into a knot.

The ends are tucked under the knot and, if need be, can be fastened with tape.

Butterfly

To gift-wrap this bottle you need three sheets of wrapping paper.

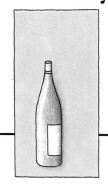 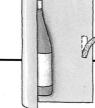  

Wrap bottle into the paper and secure the sides and the bottom with tape as shown.

Twist the portion that extends beyond the bottle into a spiral resembling a rope.

Bend the rope over and fasten it to the side of the bottle with tape.

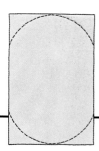 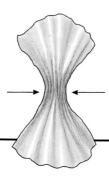 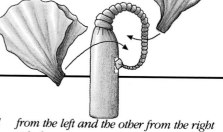

On the second and third piece of paper sketch an outline, as shown, and cut along this line.

Pull the paper together in the middle and arrange the folds evenly without creasing.

Fold the paper in half to create butterfly wings. Attach the wings to the bottle, one

from the left and the other from the right side, by pulling them through the attached rope. Fasten them with tape.

A Soft Touch

Advanced students can show off their talents by trying their hands at this unusual creation. Successfully done, it will demonstrate an ability to sculpt with paper: Masterfully rounded edges and soft flowing lines without creases or pleats require talent. Plastic-coated paper is best for this figure. Practise! In time, you will be able to master this project.

Placing a Bow

The bow remains by far the most popular decoration for a present. The use of one bow or of many changes the appearance of your present in the same way that the geometrical arrangements of different elements changes the appearance of a construction design. This is demonstrated in the seven sketches on the next two pages. One box takes on a different character by simply changing the position of the bow. The harmony between color and material in both the wrapping paper (or gift box) and the ribbon are the focal point. It will show your talent and imagination. The drawings demonstrate the individual steps of the technique and the different possibilities in placing the bow(s).

One bow in the center of the box; follow the steps.

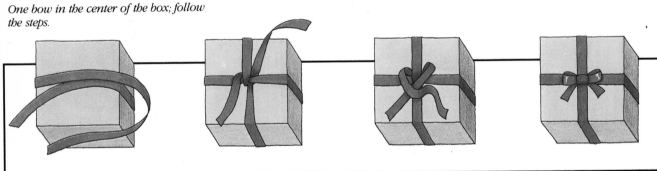

One bow at the edge; follow steps.

Bows at the corners; follow steps.

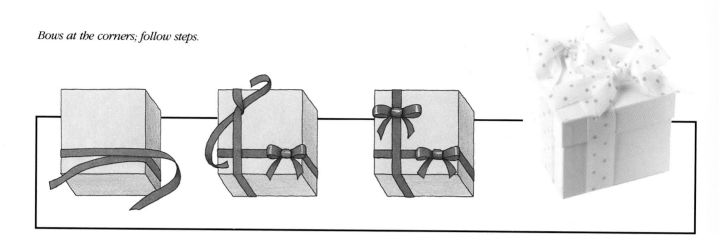

Ribbon on the diagonal; follow steps.

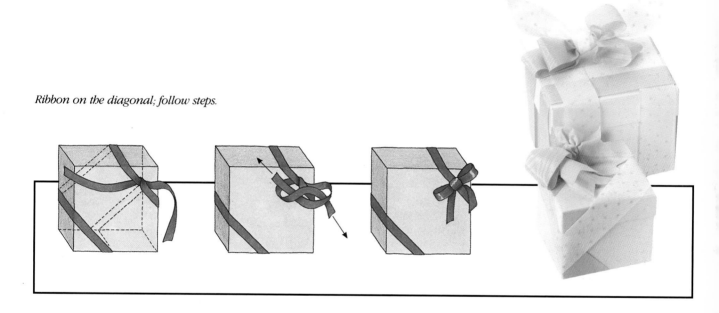

Bows all over; follow steps.

33

Bottle Parade

When you cannot afford to spend much on a gift, creative gift-wrapping will save the day. You can easily make a "big splash" with an inexpensive gift. Hidden here are wine bottles which have often been the solution to the gift question, when a sudden invitation came up.

To show how much fun one can have with a little gift like this, we decorated one bottle with braids, and one, humorously, with long ringlets! Plastic-coated paper or stiff packaging paper is needed, both of which require a little skill in handling.

Note the wonderful contrast between the stiff texture of the paper and the lightness of the feathers, a contrast underscored by the combination of colors. Copy these samples with their many folding techniques or create your own. You will have as much fun decorating your gift as your host will have receiving it.

Hiding Bottles

Wrapping paper along with accessories give a present its distinctive character. The same gift wrapped in a different "coat" would have a totally different appearance.

A gift is unassuming when using solid and cool colors and a rigid, stiff paper. Now add just a feather or two and the same gift takes on an air of elegance and whimsy.

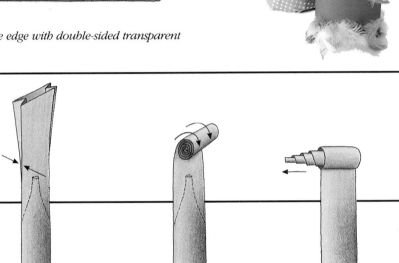

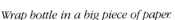

Wrap bottle in a big piece of paper.

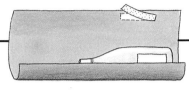

Secure edge with double-sided transparent tape.

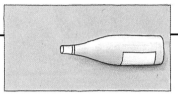

Fold paper at the bottom of the bottle and secure with tape.

Crease the sides of the paper that extends beyond the bottle and fold together.

Roll paper down as shown.

Pull out the tip and fasten with glue.

This bottle is wrapped in plastic-coated paper. It is not an easy paper to work with, since it can be unwieldy and is difficult to crease or fold. It is possible, however, to create a flowing, gentle form with this paper. In this case, the only contrast is a wide plastic ribbon in a contrasting color that has been braided.

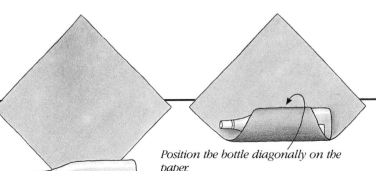

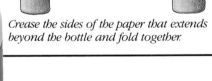

Position the bottle diagonally on the paper.

Wrap bottle to the middle of the paper as shown.

This is a very simple but attractive method for a bottle wrap. However, plastic-coated paper has to be used since many cuts have to be made and paper of less strength would tear.

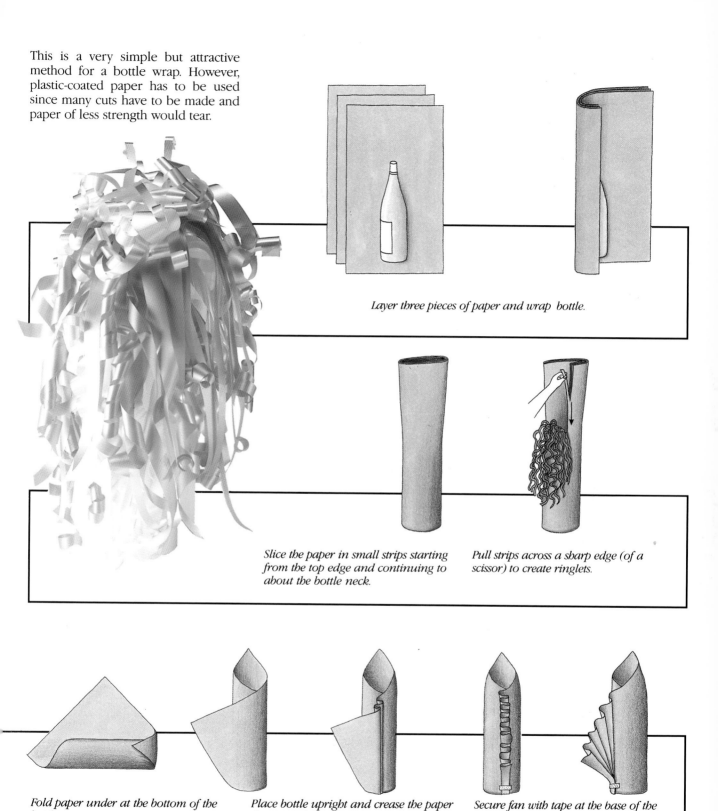

Layer three pieces of paper and wrap bottle.

Slice the paper in small strips starting from the top edge and continuing to about the bottle neck.

Pull strips across a sharp edge (of a scissor) to create ringlets.

Fold paper under at the bottom of the bottle.

Place bottle upright and crease the paper that extends beyond the side of the bottle in accordion fashion.

Secure fan with tape at the base of the bottle and pull away from the bottle.

The Individual Touch

Give the gift that you have so lovingly wrapped a special touch. We have chosen a few examples on these two pages:

A bottle wrapped in ordinary paper is topped with a braid of angel-hair.

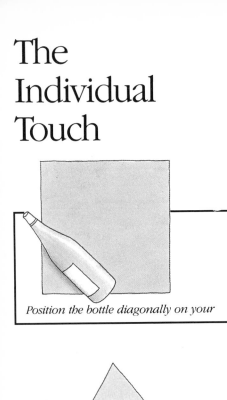

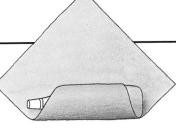

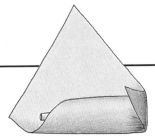

Position the bottle diagonally on your

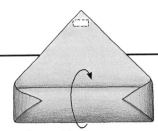

wrapping paper and roll it up halfway.

Fold both ends inside and secure.

Attach angel-hair.

Braid hair with tie end with ribbon.

If you have wide enough ribbon you do not necessarily need wrapping paper. Here is a very quick and decorative way to show off your gift.

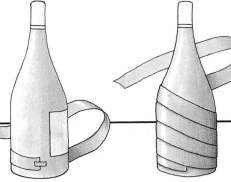

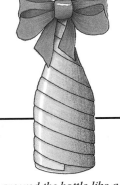

Start at the bottom and secure ribbon with transparent tape.

Wrap your ribbon around the bottle like a bandage, as shown. Secure end and attach a double bow.

If you have any very fancy wrapping paper on hand try this method. A "wrapping-enthusiast" can go all out. Grenzen gesetzt.

The gift will be special when wrapped in these wonderfully printed papers, with all the curls as an added attraction.

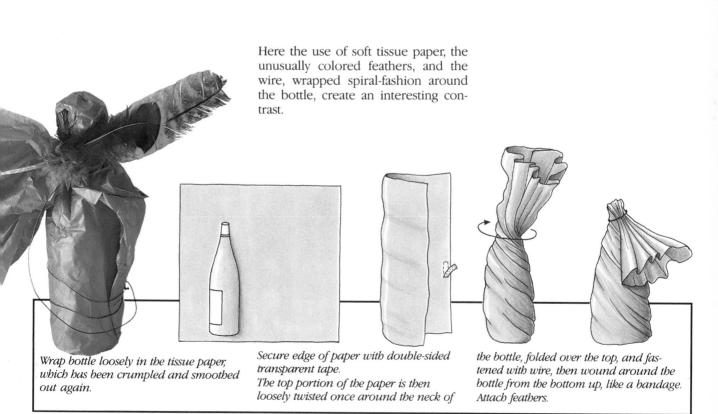

Layer the wrapping paper. Wrap as shown.

Secure edge of the paper with double-sided transparent tape.

Take a pair of pinking shears and cut the paper that extends over the bottle in small strips; let them cascade.

Here the use of soft tissue paper, the unusually colored feathers, and the wire, wrapped spiral-fashion around the bottle, create an interesting contrast.

Wrap bottle loosely in the tissue paper, which has been crumpled and smoothed out again.

Secure edge of paper with double-sided transparent tape.
The top portion of the paper is then loosely twisted once around the neck of

the bottle, folded over the top, and fastened with wire, then wound around the bottle from the bottom up, like a bandage. Attach feathers.

Two Bottles in a Blanket

Want to drop a hint on your next date? Wrap two small bottles of champagne in one sheet of wrapping paper and see if it registers!

Note: Remember, when you position the bottles on the wrapping paper leave space, equivalent to the combined width of the bottoms of these two bottles, between them.

Also: Ask for help, when wrapping; it is not easy to wrap two bottles at the same time.

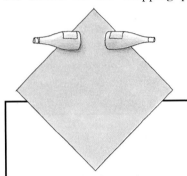

Position both bottles, as shown, on a piece of paper.

Wrap both at the same time and secure ends with transparent tape.

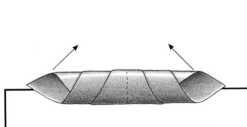

Do not fold the ends of the paper.

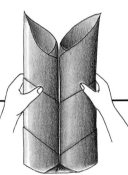

Set bottles upright so that they touch each other, then tie together with wire.

If tissue paper is used, gently pull the paper out into a bow and cut edges with pinking shears.

Or decorate with a bow of your choice.

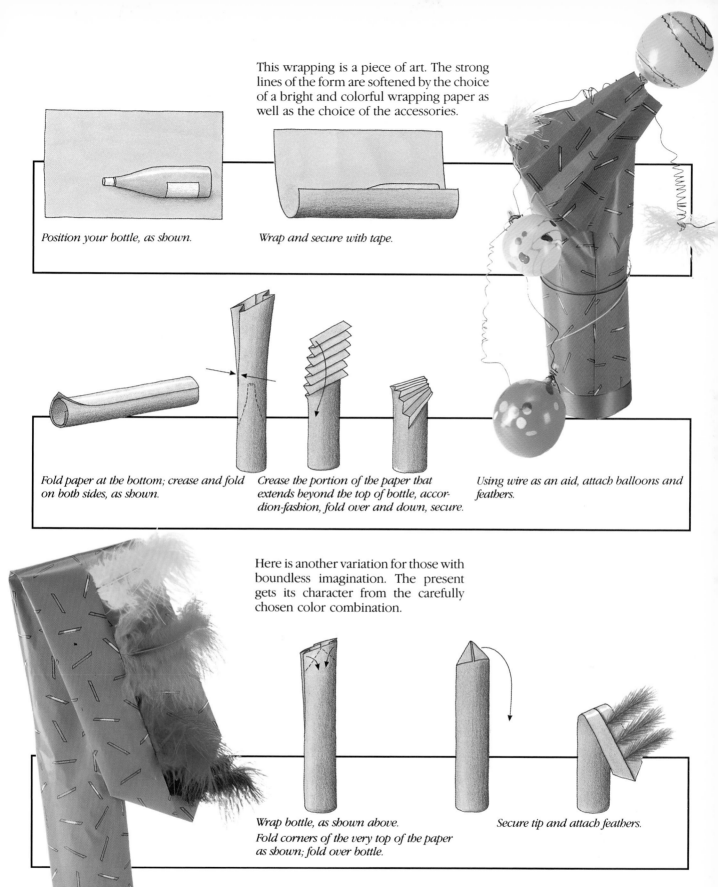

This wrapping is a piece of art. The strong lines of the form are softened by the choice of a bright and colorful wrapping paper as well as the choice of the accessories.

Position your bottle, as shown.

Wrap and secure with tape.

Fold paper at the bottom; crease and fold on both sides, as shown.

Crease the portion of the paper that extends beyond the top of bottle, accordion-fashion, fold over and down, secure.

Using wire as an aid, attach balloons and feathers.

Here is another variation for those with boundless imagination. The present gets its character from the carefully chosen color combination.

Wrap bottle, as shown above.
Fold corners of the very top of the paper as shown; fold over bottle.

Secure tip and attach feathers.

41

Wrap It in a Shirt!

The form of a shirt allows you to hide many shapes: round ones, skinny ones, flat ones and square ones! And there are many different kinds of shirts to choose from: There are tuxedo shirts with cummerbunds; those that show off a bow tie; those with lace tops and frilly bows; some that are casual and sporty. Whatever form of shirt you choose, you can be sure that your present will stand out.

The unusual effect will be achieved by the choice of paper and accessories. For instance, the buttons and the glitter give both tuxedo shirts their character and the "Happy Birthday" shirt gets its by way of fancy laces.

43

Dressing up a Bottle

It is important to note that you don't have to be a specialist in order to dress (up) a bottle. It will only take a few minutes. Just make sure that every crease and fold is executed with care and precision.

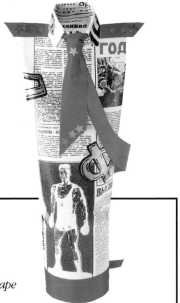

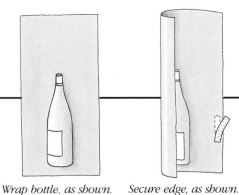

Wrap bottle, as shown. *Secure edge, as shown.* *Pull paper slightly apart, above the tape and secure.*

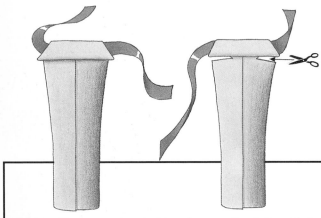

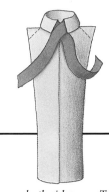

Fold top like a seam; insert ribbon for bow tie as shown; glue, or secure with double-sided transparent tape.

Carefully cut below seam on both sides about 1/3 towards the middle.

To shape shoulders, crease corners above cut and fold twice inside and secure.

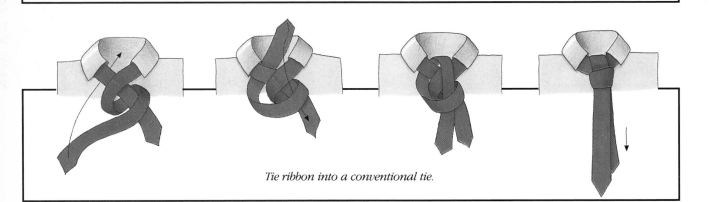

Tie ribbon into a conventional tie.

Here are more novel ways to wrap a bottle. With a bit of skill and imagination your gift can become a small work of art. As mentioned before, with the right choice of paper you can match the occasion of the party or you may want to give a hint as to the contents of the gift (e.g., Russian vodka wrapped in a page from *Pravda*). Small gift items can be attached to the outside of the wrapping with a piece of wire.

A Bottle in a Tuxedo

This is also a practical method for wrapping a book, a record or certain articles of clothing; in short, it works well with all rectangular and flat boxes.

The appearance of the wrapped package can easily be varied. Again: It is the choice of paper, the combination of color for the accessories such as buttons, bow tie, suspenders, cummerbund, etc., that will allow you to create the right wrapping for a given situation and for a given host.

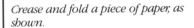

Crease and fold a piece of paper, as shown.

Secure the fold with transparent tape, as shown. Position and wrap your gift box.

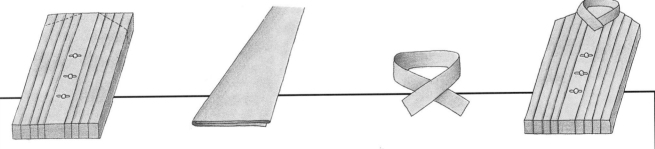

Fold and secure ends, as shown; attach buttons.

For the collar: Fold a piece of paper three times like a seam.

Form a collar, cut to size and attach.

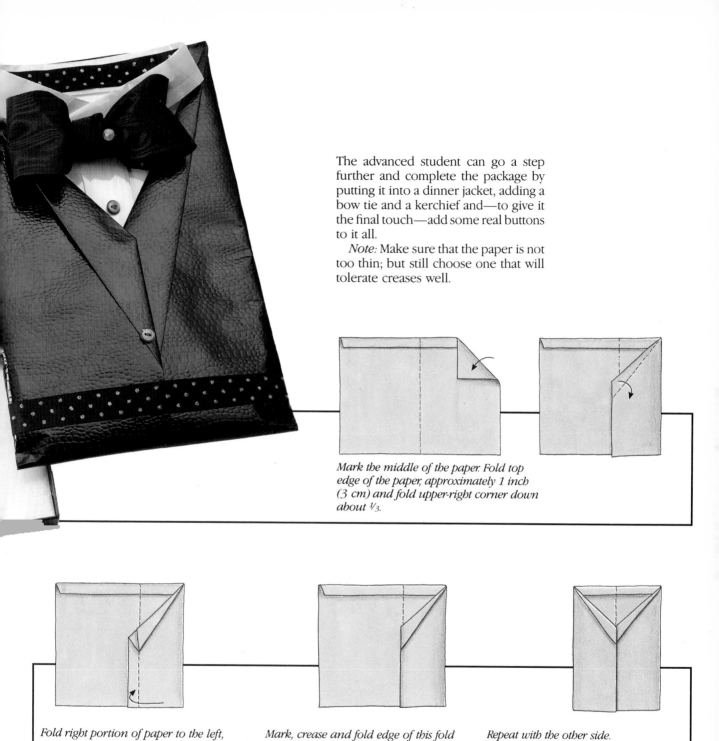

The advanced student can go a step further and complete the package by putting it into a dinner jacket, adding a bow tie and a kerchief and—to give it the final touch—add some real buttons to it all.

Note: Make sure that the paper is not too thin; but still choose one that will tolerate creases well.

Mark the middle of the paper. Fold top edge of the paper, approximately 1 inch (3 cm) and fold upper-right corner down about $^1/_3$.

Fold right portion of paper to the left, slightly past the midline. Mark, crease and fold edge down, as shown.

Mark, crease and fold edge of this fold down, as shown.

Repeat with the other side.

Attach button to your jacket.

Accessories

As you become familiar with this new way of wrapping gifts, you will learn where to find the necessary items for your project.

You want the following on hand: Glitter, small adhesive-backed stars, tinsel, a variety of ornaments, angel-hair, copper wire, feathers, a variety of beads, as well as sequins and confetti; an assortment of punched-out numbers, ornaments, and decorative paper coasters, and more. All these items are as important for your creations as an assortment of colors is for a painter.

Don't limit yourself to the obvious shops, in looking for these items. Stationery shops and florists can be treasure troves.

Remember that often the most artistic and esthetic results are due to the combination of not only different but sometimes contrasting accessories.

49

Decorations for Every Occasion

Here are some examples of how to dress up a gift box to match any occasion. The silver gift box pictured on these two pages changes its face every time we changed the decoration, for example, a red heart conveys romance, while numbers tell a realistic story. (Numbers are now available in every conceivable size, material, and color). Feathers attached with wire stand up tall and proud, while the use of angel-hair suggests softness and tenderness.

As you shop for these items be on the lookout for the unusual. Odds and ends you collect, such as pipe cleaners, will solve many a problem. They are not only very practical, they are also decorative.

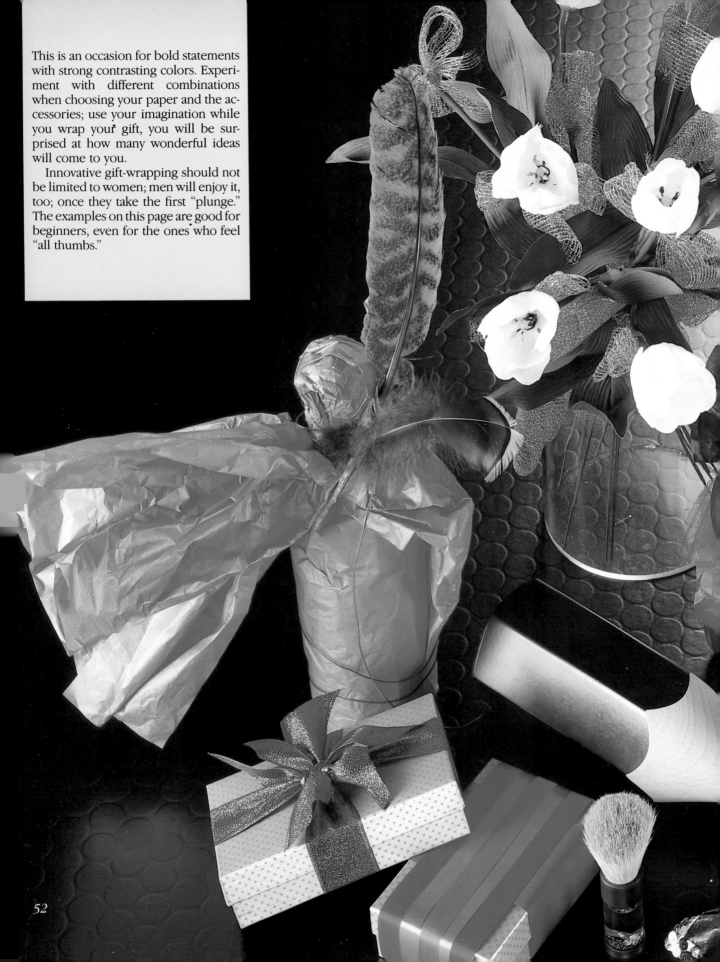

This is an occasion for bold statements with strong contrasting colors. Experiment with different combinations when choosing your paper and the accessories; use your imagination while you wrap your gift, you will be surprised at how many wonderful ideas will come to you.

Innovative gift-wrapping should not be limited to women; men will enjoy it, too; once they take the first "plunge." The examples on this page are good for beginners, even for the ones who feel "all thumbs."

Cherry Blossom *Time*

54

This is a wonderful example of how to capture the spirit of spring. We used soft tissue paper, bows, and accessories, and chose colors that complement each other. The gifts have taken center stage and are surrounded by decorations that honor the theme of the party. Take note of the many differently textured materials that have been used, and how the colors pull everything together.

Spring Is Here

Here is still another example, showing how the choice of colors creates a harmonious theme. This gift wrapper successfully combined different textured materials to create the softness and newness of spring.

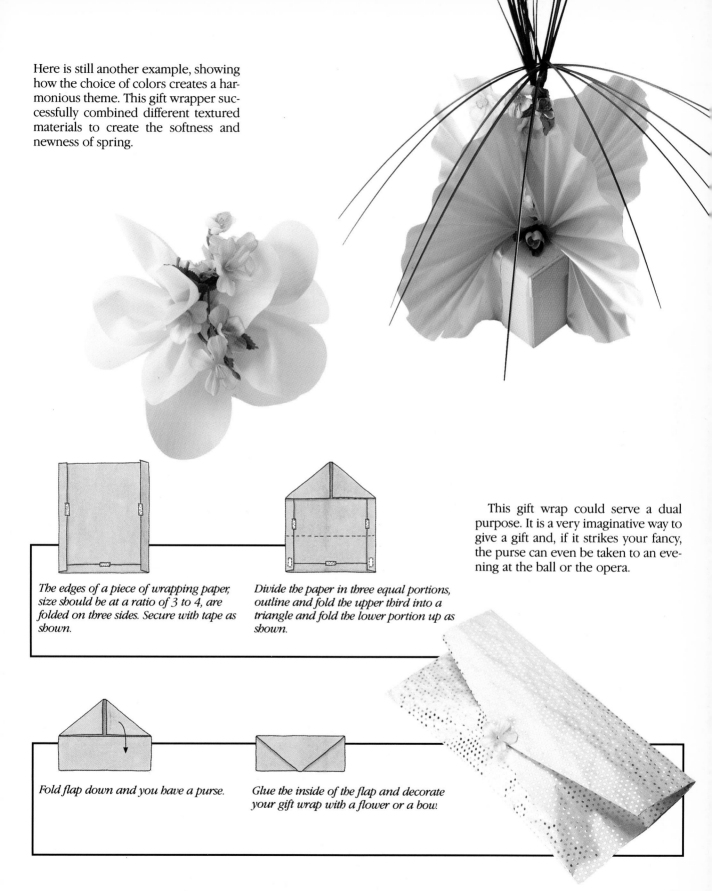

The edges of a piece of wrapping paper, size should be at a ratio of 3 to 4, are folded on three sides. Secure with tape as shown.

Divide the paper in three equal portions, outline and fold the upper third into a triangle and fold the lower portion up as shown.

This gift wrap could serve a dual purpose. It is a very imaginative way to give a gift and, if it strikes your fancy, the purse can even be taken to an evening at the ball or the opera.

Fold flap down and you have a purse.

Glue the inside of the flap and decorate your gift wrap with a flower or a bow.

It's Christmas

Another wonderful time for gift-giving is Christmas. We thought it worthwhile to show that not every gift must be wrapped in paper. One or two accessories are often all that is needed to enhance a gift. The little teddy bear, for instance, looks proud with his big red bow—nothing needs to be added. And in the case of the box with the angel wings, to position them on top of the angel-hair seems appropriate.

Wrapping for Christmas

These Christmas packages tell about the love and care of the donor, by the way they have been wrapped. The search for the accessories alone took much thought, as did the wrapping paper, lace ribbons, and the little ornamentation, not to mention the wonderful arrangement of them.

The little Santa Claus climbing up on a rope is a joyful sight.

Here a small package is decorated with angel-hair and wings.

These wrappings are truly little works of art. They are enhanced by a star-shaped platform that acts as background and is liberally sprinkled with glitter. The small folding-trees add another special touch.

Little bells have been attached to the corner of this package to provide a three-dimensional look. The bells were made from the same paper as the wrapping paper.

Easter Eggs

The table and window decorations displayed here are gaining more and more popularity. They have been made out of the same material. Often people do not unwrap the gifts immediately. They would rather wait and enjoy the pretty decorated packages throughout the Easter holidays.

Easter Bows

Yellow is one of the colors of Easter. We made a whole wreath out of yellow ribbon, with a touch of contrasting color added.

A touch of the season is created by adding a bunch of little yellow ribbons to a pure white pillow-wrap. A touch of glitter spray can be added.

The polka-dot flower is, like the wreath, a wonderful gift for the host and adds a decorative touch to the house during the Easter holiday.

Emphasis on Feathers

The voluminous bow, made of wide Poly-ribbon, has a featherlike appearance and enhances a gift that is wrapped in yellow wrapping paper.

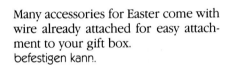

Many accessories for Easter come with wire already attached for easy attachment to your gift box.
befestigen kann.

Easter is a special time to decorate with not only figures, such as chicks, rabbits, ducklings, but also with eggs and nests and feathers. All of these can be purchased in different sizes and made of different materials.

Prime occasions for gift-giving are weddings. Here we combined black and white. But the choice of color is one of preference. Accessories will make your gift-wrapping special.

Mesh, apple blossoms, small mirrors on wires, lace ribbons, feathers, a string of beads; all are part of these wonderful creations.

The gift for the groom is decorated with a huge bow, made out of wrapping paper and attached to a gift box that is wrapped like a tuxedo.

Weddings are special occasions for very special gifts. So—let your imagination take over and don't be afraid to create your very own gift-wrap version—one that best expresses your good wishes for the lucky couple.

Wedding Bells Are

Ringing

Congratulations!

Golden and silver wedding anniversaries are important occasions for gift-giving. They call for a bit of imagination in order to avoid the commonplace.

Numbers, to match the number of years that have passed, are easily available.

Wrap presents in honor of the day in the appropriate paper and add gold-leaf numbers; and/or big oversized bows or many small ones, from different materials or made from the same; and add feathers and/or leaves. All are a part of the creation of a gift box that matches the special occasion.

Young, dynamic, and strongheaded: That is what being a teen or in one's early twenties is all about. And that should hold true for the presents we give them.

Here we drop all the conventional ways of wrapping presents. We create small works of art by making use of the many different smooth and glossy, asymmetrical, colorful accessories. We turn gift boxes into something special, something that will match the recipients personality. The accessories consist of lots of florist wire in every conceivable color and shape. The wire can be wrapped around pencils and bounce freely away from the gift box.

For the Young Adult

Daring Colors

The motto here is: Be bold. Have courage. Everything goes. Take the unusual and add it to your creation—like the little umbrellas that up to now were decorating hot weather drinks. Then there are paperclips: Take them out of the office! The original use is turned around. Ribbon is not for tying bows or wrapping around packages anymore; you make a sculpture out of them.

Wrapping paper should have solid, strong, clear, and bold colors of yellows, reds, pink and so forth.

The most important tool is one pair of household scissors, so that cuts are clear and precise. A pair of pinking shears for decorative cuts is also useful.

Red and Black

Here we mixed classical colors into new creations. For accessories, we used spiraled ribbons, a tie and a bow tie, together with a mess of strings and red wire. To describe these combinations does not do justice to the effect they have on your gift box. No directions given, they are not necessary. You must let your imagination soar and make use of your talents. You can do it!!!

The black and red color combination and the different qualities in the material will allow you to decorate boldly and with flair. Your wrapped gift boxes will express your imagination and daring. This is no time to be shy.

New York is a symbol for effervescence, for vibrant colors, and for gigantic architecture. These pages try to convey some of that spirit; we tried to transform it to the wrappings of the gift boxes. Neon colored material, glitter, and pop colors will make your gift boxes art objects. Classical forms next to glistening high rise façades are not contradictions but are life-confirming and coexist, giving a voice to the past and a sense of the future. Feathers give the whole a sense of lightness and are another means to create contrast.

NEW YORK

NEW YORK

American life is mirrored in brilliant, glowing, and star-studded colors and shapes. Courage for the extreme is the basis for this decorating method. Metallic paper, nylon net, extra-wide ribbon and feathers are the ingredients for this American cocktail. The box of candies is simply wrapped in a colorful combination of brilliant paper and accessories. The Sioux Indian is a bit more difficult to make. It is a bottle hidden in red pleated paper and the hair is red angel-hair, braided and decorated with a contrasting green feather. The little box behind the Indian is another example of the effectiveness of contrasting colors and material: Wide ribbon, spiral-shaped florist wire and a nylon net bursting in its bright yellow color. If the shape of a gift box is square it can be dressed up in asymmetrical pleats that are highlighted with glitter. Again, the play in contrast is intriguing; here we set wide ribbon against the lightness of a feather.

INDEX

accessories, 48–49
accordion creases, 22–23, 41, 46
American life, 78–79
angel-hair, 38
anniversaries, golden and silver, 68–69

bells, 61
bottles, 34, 35, 36–37, 44, 45, 46, 53
bow placement, 32–33
bows, 12, 15, 24–25, 26–27, 32, 38, 43, 44
bow tie, 44

cherry blossoms, 54–55
Christmas, 58–61
colors, daring, 72–73
creasing, 18
crunching and crumpling, 19

decorations, 50–51
dress envelope, 57

Easter, 62–65

fabric, 10
fan, 20–21, 36–37, 54, 55, 57
fan bow, 26
feathers, 39, 41, 47, 49
florist's wire, 11
folding, 14, 18

materials, 8–9, 29, 36–37

New York, New York, 76–77
numbers, 50–51

paper bows, 30–31, 40
papers, 9, 10, 16, 35

red and black, 74–75
ribbon, 10, 24, 26–27, 28, 36–37, 38–39

Santa Claus, 60
shears, pinking, 11, 39
shirt wrapping, 42–43, 44, 46–47
spring decorations, 56–57

tape, transparent, 11, 36, 37, 39
teddy bear, 58, 61
ties, 44
tissue paper, 40
tools, 11
tuxedo, 46–47

umbrellas, 49

weddings, 66–67

young adult, 70–71